PIANO · VOCAL · GUITAR

Country 35 Standards

MT. GILEAD PUBLIC LIBRARY

WITHDRAWN

ISBN 0-634-02882-0

HAL·LEONARD®
CORPORATION
7777 W. BLUEMOUND RD. P.O. BOX 13819 MILWAUKEE, WI 53213

For all works contained herein:
Unauthorized copying, arranging, adapting, recording or public performance is an infringement of copyright.
Infringers are liable under the law.

Visit Hal Leonard Online at
www.halleonard.com

CONTENTS

ALL THE GOLD IN CALIFORNIA

Words and Music by
LARRY GATLIN

© 1979 TEMI COMBINE INC. and SONGS OF UNIVERSAL, INC.
All Rights for TEMI COMBINE INC. Controlled by COMBINE MUSIC CORP. and Administered by EMI BLACKWOOD MUSIC INC.
All Rights Reserved   International Copyright Secured   Used by Permission

To Coda

it don't mat-ter at all__ where you've played__ be-fore__ Cal-i-for-nia's a brand new__

game._____ Try-in' to be a he-ro___ wind-ing up a

ze-ro___ can scar a man for-ev-er_____ right down to your

soul._____ Liv-ing on the spot-light___ can kill a man__

ALWAYS ON MY MIND

Words and Music by WAYNE THOMPSON,
MARK JAMES and JOHNNY CHRISTOPHER

© 1971 (Renewed 1999), 1979 SCREEN GEMS-EMI MUSIC INC. and SEBANINE MUSIC, INC.
All Rights Controlled and Administered by SCREEN GEMS-EMI MUSIC INC.
All Rights Reserved   International Copyright Secured   Used by Permission

ANGEL OF THE MORNING

Words and Music by
CHIP TAYLOR

© 1967 (Renewed 1995) EMI BLACKWOOD MUSIC INC.
All Rights Reserved   International Copyright Secured   Used by Permission

BLUE BAYOU

Words and Music by ROY ORBISON
and JOE MELSON

Copyright © 1961 (Renewed 1989) by Acuff-Rose Music, Inc., Barbara Orbison Music Company, Orbi-Lee Music and R-Key Darkus Music
All Rights Reserved   Used by Permission

BLUE EYES CRYING IN THE RAIN

Words and Music by
FRED ROSE

Copyright © 1945 (Renewed 1973) by Milene Music, Inc.
All Rights Reserved   Used by Permission

COWARD OF THE COUNTY

Words and Music by ROGER BOWLING
and BILLY EDD WHEELER

Copyright © 1979 by Careers-BMG Music Publishing, Inc. and Universal - MCA Music Publishing, A Division of Universal Studios, Inc.
International Copyright Secured   All Rights Reserved

some - one for ev - 'ry one___ and Tom - my's love___ was Beck - y,___

In her arms___ he did - n't have___ to prove he was a man.___

___ One day while he was work - in'___ the

Gat - lin boys___ came call - in', They took turns___ at Beck - y,___

24

As his tears fell on his dad-dy's face, he heard these words a-gain:

"Prom-ise me son, _____ not to do _____ the things I've done, Walk a-way from trou-ble if you can. _____

It won't mean you're weak _____ if you turn _____

BOOT SCOOTIN' BOOGIE

Words and Music by
RONNIE DUNN

Copyright © 1991 Sony/ATV Songs LLC
All Rights Administered by Sony/ATV Music Publishing, 8 Music Square West, Nashville, TN 37203
International Copyright Secured   All Rights Reserved

CRYING

Words and Music by ROY ORBISON
and JOE MELSON

Copyright © 1961 (Renewed 1989) by Acuff-Rose Music, Inc., Barbara Orbison Music Company, Orbi-Lee Music and R-Key Darkus Music
All Rights Reserved   Used by Permission

DISTANT DRUMS

Words and Music by
CINDY WALKER

© 1963 (Renewed 1991) TEMI COMBINE INC.
All Rights Controlled by COMBINE MUSIC CORP. and Administered by EMI BLACKWOOD MUSIC INC.
All Rights Reserved   International Copyright Secured   Used by Permission

ELVIRA

Words and Music by
DALLAS FRAZIER

Copyright © 1965 (Renewed 1993) by Acuff-Rose Music, Inc.
All Rights Reserved   Used by Permission

Verse 2. Tonight I'm gonna meet her
At the hungry house cafe
And I'm gonna give her all the love I can
She's gonna jump and holler
'Cause I saved up my last two dollar
And we're gonna search and find that preacher man
Chorus

FOR THE GOOD TIMES

Words and Music by
KRIS KRISTOFFERSON

Copyright © 1968 by Careers-BMG Music Publishing, Inc.
Copyright Renewed
International Copyright Secured   All Rights Reserved

FOLSOM PRISON BLUES

Words and Music by
JOHN R. CASH

Moderately (not too slow)

hear the train a-com-in'; it's roll-in' 'round the bend, And
I was just a ba-by my ma-ma told me son,_____

I ain't seen the sun-shine since I don't know when. I'm
al-ways be a good boy; don't ev-er play with guns," But I

© 1956 (Renewed 1984) HOUSE OF CASH, INC. (BMI)/Administered by BUG MUSIC
All Rights Reserved   Used by Permission

3. I bet there's rich folks eatin' in a fancy dining car.
   They're prob'ly drinkin' coffee and smokin' big cigars,
   But I know I had it comin', I know I can't be free,
   But those people keep a-movin', and that's what tortures me.

4. Well, if they freed me from this prison, if that railroad train was mine,
   I bet I'd move on over a little farther down the line,
   Far from Folsom Prison, that's where I want to stay,
   And I'd let that lonesome whistle blow my blues away.

FRIENDS IN LOW PLACES

Words and Music by DEWAYNE BLACKWELL
and EARL BUD LEE

Copyright © 1990 by Careers-BMG Music Publishing, Inc. and Sony/ATV Tunes LLC
All Rights on behalf of Sony/ATV Tunes LLC Administered by Sony/ATV Music Publishing, 8 Music Square West, Nashville, TN 37203
International Copyright Secured   All Rights Reserved

52

THE GAMBLER

Words and Music by
DON SCHLITZ

Copyright © 1977 Sony/ATV Tunes LLC
All Rights Administered by Sony/ATV Music Publishing, 8 Music Square West, Nashville, TN 37203
International Copyright Secured   All Rights Reserved

57

'em, know when to walk___ a-way___ and know when to run.___

___ You nev-er count your mon-ey when you're sit-tin' at the ta-

-ble there'll be time e-nough___ for count-in' when the deal-in's

done

MT. GILEAD PUBLIC LIBRARY

HARD ROCK BOTTOM OF YOUR HEART

Words and Music by
HUGH PRESTWOOD

Moderately fast Country

Since the day _____ I was led ___ to ___ temp -
_____ that we led built ___ is ___ still ___

ta - tion, ___ and in weak - ness ___ did
stand - ing. ___ Its foun - da - tion ___ is

Copyright © 1989 by Careers-BMG Music Publishing, Inc. and Hugh Prestwood Music
All Rights Administered by Careers-BMG Music Publishing, Inc.
International Copyright Secured   All Rights Reserved

D.S. al Coda

(Solo ends) **And I keep**

CODA

To the hard __ rock bot - tom of __ your heart,__

to the hard __ rock bot -

- tom _____ of your heart. _____

Repeat and Fade

GEORGIA ON MY MIND

Words by STUART GORRELL
Music by HOAGY CARMICHAEL

Copyright © 1930 by Peermusic Ltd.
Copyright Renewed
International Copyright Secured   All Rights Reserved

HE'LL HAVE TO GO

Words and Music by JOE ALLISON
and AUDREY ALLISON

© 1959 (Renewed 1987) BEECHWOOD MUSIC CORP.
All Rights Reserved   International Copyright Secured   Used by Permission

blind, make up your mind; I've got to know. _____ Should I

hang up ___ or will you tell him ___ he'll have to go? _____ You can't

say the words I want to hear while you're with an-oth-er man. If you

want me, an-swer "Yes" or "No;" dar-ling, I will un-der-stand. Put your

HELP ME MAKE IT THROUGH THE NIGHT

Words and Music by
KRIS KRISTOFFERSON

© 1970 (Renewed 1998) TEMI COMBINE INC.
All Rights Controlled by COMBINE MUSIC CORP. and Administered by EMI BLACKWOOD MUSIC INC.
All Rights Reserved   International Copyright Secured   Used by Permission

HEY, GOOD LOOKIN'

Words and Music by
HANK WILLIAMS

Copyright © 1951 (Renewed 1975) by Acuff-Rose Music, Inc. and Hiriam Music in the U.S.A.
All Rights for Hiriam Music Administered by Rightsong Music Inc.
All Rights outside the U.S.A. Controlled by Acuff-Rose Music, Inc.
All Rights Reserved   Used by Permission

danc - in's free, so if you wan - na have fun come a - long with me____
cov - ered with age____ 'Cause I'm writ - in' your name down on ev - 'ry page____

C

Hey, Good Look - in' What - cha got cook - in'
Hey, Good Look - in' What - cha got cook - in'

D7   **G7**   **C**

How's a - bout cook - in' some - thin' up with me.____
How's a - bout cook - in' some - thin' up with

C   **F**   **C**

I'm me.____

HERE YOU COME AGAIN

Words by CYNTHIA WEIL
Music by BARRY MANN

© 1977 SCREEN GEMS-EMI MUSIC INC. and SUMMERHILL SONGS INC.
All Rights Controlled and Administered by SCREEN GEMS-EMI MUSIC INC.
All Rights Reserved   International Copyright Secured   Used by Permission

I BELIEVE IN YOU

Words and Music by ROGER COOK
and SAM HOGIN

© 1980 SCREEN GEMS-EMI MUSIC INC.
All Rights Reserved International Copyright Secured Used by Permission

I CAN LOVE YOU LIKE THAT

Words and Music by MARIBETH DERRY,
JENNIFER KIMBALL and STEVE DIAMOND

Copyright © 1995 Criterion Music Corp., EMI Full Keel Music Co., Friends And Angels Music, Second Wave Music and Diamond Cuts
All Rights for Friends And Angels Music Controlled and Administered by EMI Full Keel Music Co.
All Rights for Second Wave Music Administered by Universal - MCA Music Publishing, A Division of Universal Studios, Inc.
All Rights for Diamond Cuts Administered by Zomba Enterprises, Inc.
All Rights Reserved   Used by Permission

I CAN'T STOP LOVING YOU

Words and Music by
DON GIBSON

Copyright © 1958 (Renewed 1985) by Acuff-Rose Music, Inc.
All Rights Reserved   Used by Permission

I LOVE A RAINY NIGHT

Words and Music by EDDIE RABBITT,
EVEN STEVENS and DAVID MALLOY

Moderately Bright

© 1980 SCREEN GEMS-EMI MUSIC INC.
All Rights Reserved International Copyright Secured Used by Permission

I WALK THE LINE

Words and Music by
JOHN R. CASH

Moderate

1. I keep a close watch on this heart of mine.
   ver - y eas - y to be true.

I keep my eyes wide o - pen all the
I find my - self a - lone when each day is

time. I keep the ends out for the tie that
through. Yes, I'll ad - mit out that I'm a fool for

© 1956 (Renewed 1984) HOUSE OF CASH, INC. (BMI)/Administered by BUG MUSIC
All Rights Reserved   Used by Permission

3. As sure as night is dark and day is light,
   I keep you on my mind both day and night.
   And happiness I've known proves that it's right.
   Because you're mine I Walk The Line.

4. You've got a way to keep me on your side.
   You give me cause for love that I can't hide.
   For you I know I'd even try to turn the tide.
   Because you're mine I Walk The Line.

5. I keep a close watch on this heart of mine.
   I keep my eyes wide open all the time.
   I keep the ends out for the tie that binds.
   Because you're mine I Walk The Line.

IT'S YOUR LOVE

Words and Music by
STEPHONY E. SMITH

© 1996 EMI BLACKWOOD MUSIC INC.
All Rights Reserved   International Copyright Secured   Used by Permission

THE KEEPER OF THE STARS

Words and Music by KAREN STALEY,
DANNY MAYO and DICKEY LEE

Copyright © 1994 by Careers-BMG Music Publishing, Inc., Sixteen Stars Music, Murrah Music Corporation,
Universal - Songs Of PolyGram International, Inc. and Pal Time Music
International Copyright Secured   All Rights Reserved

LOOKIN' FOR LOVE

Words and Music by WANDA MALLETTE,
PATTI RYAN and BOB MORRISON

© 1980 TEMI COMBINE INC. and SOUTHERN DAYS MUSIC (administered by COPYRIGHT MANAGEMENT INTERNATIONAL)
All Rights for TEMI COMBINE INC. Controlled by MUSIC CITY MUSIC INC. and Administered by EMI APRIL MUSIC INC.
All Rights Reserved International Copyright Secured Used by Permission

G

Then you came a-knock-in' at my heart's door;___ you're

Em   F#m   G   A

ev - 'ry - thing_ I've been look - in' for._____

D.S. al Coda

_ No more

CODA   G

you,   oh

Em   A   D

you;   look-in' for love ____   in all ___ the wrong plac - es;

LOVE WITHOUT END, AMEN

Words and Music by
AARON G. BARKER

Copyright © 1990 O-Tex Music (BMI) and Bill Butler Music (BMI), 1000 18th Avenue South, Nashville, TN 37212
International Copyright Secured   All Rights Reserved

122

OH, PRETTY WOMAN

Words and Music by ROY ORBISON
and BILL DEES

Copyright © 1964 (Renewed 1992) by Acuff-Rose Music, Inc., Barbara Orbison Music Company, Orbi-Lee Music and R-Key Darkus Music
All Rights Reserved   Used by Permission

RING OF FIRE

Words and Music by MERLE KILGORE
and JUNE CARTER

Moderately Bright

Love _____ is a burn-ing thing _____
taste _____ of__ love is sweet _____

And it makes _____ a fi-ry
When_ hearts _____ like ours _

Copyright © 1962, 1963 Painted Desert Music Corporation, New York
Copyright Renewed
International Copyright Secured All Rights Reserved
Used by Permission

RELEASE ME

Words and Music by ROBERT YOUNT,
EDDIE MILLER and DUB WILLIAMS

Copyright © 1954 (Renewed 1982) by Acuff-Rose Music, Inc. and Roschelle Publishing in the U.S.A.
All Rights outside the U.S.A. Controlled by Acuff-Rose Music, Inc.
All Rights Reserved   Used by Permission

SNOWBIRD

Words and Music by
GENE MacLELLAN

© 1970 (Renewed 1998) EMI BLACKWOOD MUSIC INC.
All Rights Reserved   International Copyright Secured   Used by Permission

WHEN YOU SAY NOTHING AT ALL

Words and Music by PAUL OVERSTREET
and DON SCHLITZ

© 1988 SCREEN GEMS-EMI MUSIC INC., SCARLET MOON MUSIC, UNIVERSAL - MCA MUSIC PUBLISHING,
A Division of UNIVERSAL STUDIOS, INC. and DON SCHLITZ MUSIC
All Rights for SCARLET MOON MUSIC Administered by COPYRIGHT MANAGEMENT INTERNATIONAL
All Rights for DON SCHLITZ MUSIC Controlled and Administered by UNIVERSAL - MCA MUSIC PUBLISHING, A Division of UNIVERSAL STUDIOS, INC.
All Rights Reserved   International Copyright Secured   Used by Permission

YOU ARE MY SUNSHINE

Words and Music by JIMMIE DAVIS
and CHARLES MITCHELL

Tenderly

The oth - er night, dear, _____
love you _____
once, dear, _____

_____ as I lay sleep - ing, _____ I dreamed I
_____ and make you hap - py _____ if you will
_____ you real - ly loved me _____ and no one

held you in my arms. _____
on - ly could say come be - same. _____
else could come be - tween. _____

Copyright © 1930 by Peer International Corporation
Copyright Renewed
International Copyright Secured   All Rights Reserved

WITHDRAWN

LIBRARY